VIVIAN TENORIO

my first
gratitude journal

This journal belongs to:

_____

VIVIAN TENORIO

my first

gratitude journal

a write-in, draw-in gratitude journal for kids

BY VIVIAN TENORIO

JAV PUBLISHING

v

VIVIAN TENORIO

Cover Illustration: My Sweet Daughter
painted in art class on 09-17-04

Printed in the United Stated of America

www.viviantenorio.com

ISBN-10: 061557842X
ISBN-13: 978-0615578422

grat·i·tude [grat-i-tood]
a feeling of thankfulness or appreciation, as for gifts or favours.

I am grateful for my new bike.

☀ TODAY IS _____ , 20

I am grateful

_____

_____

I am grateful

_____

_____

I am grateful

_____

_____

I am grateful

_____

_____

 TODAY IS _____ , 20 ____

I am grateful

I am grateful

I am grateful

I am grateful

☼ TODAY IS _____ , 20 ___

No writing today. Draw a picture of what you are grateful for.

 TODAY IS _____ , 20 ____

I am grateful

_____

_____

I am grateful

_____

_____

I am grateful

_____

_____

I am grateful

_____

_____

TODAY IS _____ , 20 ____

I am grateful
_____

_____

I am grateful
_____

_____

I am grateful
_____

_____

I am grateful
_____

_____

☆ TODAY IS _____ , 20 ____

No writing today. Draw a picture of what you are
grateful for.

MY FIRST GRATITUDE JOURNAL

☼ TODAY IS _____ , 20 ___

I am grateful

_____

_____

I am grateful

_____

_____

I am grateful

_____

_____

I am grateful

_____

_____

 TODAY IS _____ , 20 _____

I am grateful

_____

_____

I am grateful

_____

_____

I am grateful

_____

_____

I am grateful

_____

_____

TODAY IS _____ , 20 ___

No writing today. Draw a picture of what you are grateful for.

 TODAY IS _____ , 20 ___

I am grateful

I am grateful

I am grateful

I am grateful

TODAY IS _____ , 20 ___

I am grateful

_____

_____

I am grateful

_____

_____

I am grateful

_____

_____

I am grateful

_____

_____

☆ TODAY IS _____ , 20 ___

No writing today. Draw a picture of what you are grateful for.

☼ TODAY IS _____ , 20

I am grateful

_____

_____

I am grateful

_____

_____

I am grateful

_____

_____

I am grateful

_____

_____

VIVIAN TENORIO

 TODAY IS _____ , 20

I am grateful

_____

_____

I am grateful

_____

_____

I am grateful

_____

_____

I am grateful

_____

_____

TODAY IS _____ , 20

No Writing today. Draw a picture of What you are grateful for.

 TODAY IS _____ , 20 ___

I am grateful

_____

_____

I am grateful

_____

_____

I am grateful

_____

_____

I am grateful

_____

_____

MY FIRST GRATITUDE JOURNAL

TODAY IS _____ , 20 ____

I am grateful

_____

_____

I am grateful

_____

_____

I am grateful

_____

_____

I am grateful

_____

_____

 TODAY IS _____ , 20 _____

I am grateful

_____

_____

I am grateful

_____

_____

I am grateful

_____

_____

I am grateful

_____

_____

TODAY IS _____ , 20

I am grateful

_____

_____

I am grateful

_____

_____

I am grateful

_____

_____

I am grateful

_____

_____

⚘ TODAY IS _____ , 20

No writing today. Draw a picture of what you are grateful for.

TODAY IS _____ , 20 _____

I am grateful

_____

_____

I am grateful

_____

_____

I am grateful

_____

_____

I am grateful

_____

_____

TODAY IS _____ , 20 ___

I am grateful

_____

_____

I am grateful

_____

_____

I am grateful

_____

_____

I am grateful

_____

_____

⭐ TODAY IS _____ , 20

No writing today. Draw a picture of what you are grateful for.

TODAY IS _____ , 20

I am grateful

_____

_____

I am grateful

_____

_____

I am grateful

_____

_____

I am grateful

_____

_____

TODAY IS _____ , 20 ____

I am grateful

_____

_____

I am grateful

_____

_____

I am grateful

_____

_____

I am grateful

_____

_____

☼ TODAY IS   , 20

No writing today. Draw a picture of what you are
grateful for.

TODAY IS _____ , 20 ___

I am grateful

_____

_____

I am grateful

_____

_____

I am grateful

_____

_____

I am grateful

_____

_____

 TODAY IS _____ , 20 ___

I am grateful

I am grateful

I am grateful

I am grateful

☆ TODAY IS _____ , 20 ____

No writing today. Draw a picture of what you are grateful for.

☀ TODAY IS _____ , 20____

I am grateful

_____

_____

I am grateful

_____

_____

I am grateful

_____

_____

I am grateful

_____

_____

☀ TODAY IS _____ , 20___

I am grateful

_____

_____

I am grateful

_____

_____

I am grateful

_____

_____

I am grateful

_____

_____

⚘ TODAY IS _____ , 20 ____

No writing today. Draw a picture of what you are grateful for.

☙ TODAY IS _____ , 20

I am grateful

_____

_____

I am grateful

_____

_____

I am grateful

_____

_____

I am grateful

_____

_____

 TODAY IS _____ , 20 ___

I am grateful

_____

_____

I am grateful

_____

_____

I am grateful

_____

_____

I am grateful

_____

_____

☀ TODAY IS _____ , 20

I am grateful

_____

_____

I am grateful

_____

_____

I am grateful

_____

_____

I am grateful

_____

_____

 TODAY IS _____ , 20

I am grateful

_____

_____

I am grateful

_____

_____

I am grateful

_____

_____

I am grateful

_____

_____

TODAY IS _____ , 20 ___

No Writing today. Draw a picture of What you are grateful for.

TODAY IS _____ , 20

I am grateful

_____

_____

I am grateful

_____

_____

I am grateful

_____

_____

I am grateful

_____

_____

☺ TODAY IS _____ , 20 ___

I am grateful

_____

_____

I am grateful

_____

_____

I am grateful

_____

_____

I am grateful

_____

_____

☆ TODAY IS _____ , 20 ___

No writing today. Draw a picture of what you are grateful for.

☀ TODAY IS _____ , 20 ____

I am grateful

_____

_____

I am grateful

_____

_____

I am grateful

_____

_____

I am grateful

_____

_____

TODAY IS _____ , 20 _____

I am grateful
_____

_____

I am grateful
_____

_____

I am grateful
_____

_____

I am grateful
_____

_____

TODAY IS _____ , 20

No writing today. Draw a picture of what you are grateful for.

 TODAY IS _____ , 20

I am grateful

_____

_____

I am grateful

_____

_____

I am grateful

_____

_____

I am grateful

_____

_____

TODAY IS _____ , 20

I am grateful

_____

_____

I am grateful

_____

_____

I am grateful

_____

_____

I am grateful

_____

_____

☆ TODAY IS _____ , 20 ___

No writing today. Draw a picture of what you are grateful for.

☀ TODAY IS _____ , 20 ____

I am grateful

_____

_____

I am grateful

_____

_____

I am grateful

_____

_____

I am grateful

_____

_____

 TODAY IS _____ , 20 ____

I am grateful

_____

_____

I am grateful

_____

_____

I am grateful

_____

_____

I am grateful

_____

_____

 TODAY IS _____ , 20

No writing today. Draw a picture of what you are grateful for.

 TODAY IS _____ , 20___

I am grateful

_____

_____

I am grateful

_____

_____

I am grateful

_____

_____

I am grateful

_____

_____

TODAY IS   , 20

I am grateful

_____

_____

I am grateful

_____

_____

I am grateful

_____

_____

I am grateful

_____

_____

 TODAY IS _____ , 20 ____

I am grateful

_____

_____

I am grateful

_____

_____

I am grateful

_____

_____

I am grateful

_____

_____

TODAY IS _____ , 20 ____

I am grateful

_____

_____

I am grateful

_____

_____

I am grateful

_____

_____

I am grateful

_____

_____

✿ TODAY IS   , 20

No writing today. Draw a picture of what you are grateful for.

TODAY IS _____ , 20 ___

I am grateful

_____

_____

I am grateful

_____

_____

I am grateful

_____

_____

I am grateful

_____

_____

TODAY IS _____ , 20 _____

I am grateful

_____

_____

I am grateful

_____

_____

I am grateful

_____

_____

I am grateful

_____

_____

☆ TODAY IS _____ , 20 ____

No Writing today. Draw a picture of What you are grateful for.

☀ TODAY IS _____ , 20 ___

I am grateful

_____

_____

I am grateful

_____

_____

I am grateful

_____

_____

I am grateful

_____

_____

TODAY IS _____ , 20 ___

I am grateful

_____

_____

I am grateful

_____

_____

I am grateful

_____

_____

I am grateful

_____

_____

✿ TODAY IS _____ , 20

No writing today. Draw a picture of what you are grateful for.

TODAY IS _____ , 20 ____

I am grateful

_____

_____

I am grateful

_____

_____

I am grateful

_____

_____

I am grateful

_____

_____

 TODAY IS _____ , 20 ____

I am grateful

_____

_____

I am grateful

_____

_____

I am grateful

_____

_____

I am grateful

_____

_____

⭐ TODAY IS _____ , 20 _____

No writing today. Draw a picture of what you are grateful for.

 TODAY IS _____ , 20 ____

I am grateful

_____

_____

I am grateful

_____

_____

I am grateful

_____

_____

I am grateful

_____

_____

TODAY IS _____ , 20___

I am grateful

_____

_____

I am grateful

_____

_____

I am grateful

_____

_____

I am grateful

_____

_____

 TODAY IS _____ , 20

No Writing today. Draw a picture of What you are grateful for.

TODAY IS _____ , 20 ____

I am grateful

_____

_____

I am grateful

_____

_____

I am grateful

_____

_____

I am grateful

_____

_____

TODAY IS _____ , 20 ___

I am grateful

_____

_____

I am grateful

_____

_____

I am grateful

_____

_____

I am grateful

_____

_____

☀ TODAY IS _____ , 20 _____

I am grateful

_____

_____

I am grateful

_____

_____

I am grateful

_____

_____

I am grateful

_____

_____

 TODAY IS _____ , 20 ___

I am grateful

_____

_____

I am grateful

_____

_____

I am grateful

_____

_____

I am grateful

_____

_____

⚘ TODAY IS _____ , 20 ___

No writing today. Draw a picture of what you are grateful for.

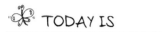 TODAY IS _____ , 20

I am grateful

_____

_____

I am grateful

_____

_____

I am grateful

_____

_____

I am grateful

_____

_____

TODAY IS _____ , 20 _____

I am grateful

_____

_____

I am grateful

_____

_____

I am grateful

_____

_____

I am grateful

_____

_____

⭐ TODAY IS _____ , 20

No writing today. Draw a picture of what you are grateful for.

☼ TODAY IS _____ , 20 ____

I am grateful

_____

_____

I am grateful

_____

_____

I am grateful

_____

_____

I am grateful

_____

_____

 TODAY IS _____ , 20 __

I am grateful

_____

_____

I am grateful

_____

_____

I am grateful

_____

_____

I am grateful

_____

_____

⚘ TODAY IS _____ , 20 ___

No writing today. Draw a picture of what you are grateful for.

 TODAY IS _____ , 20 _____

I am grateful
_____

_____

I am grateful
_____

_____

I am grateful
_____

_____

I am grateful
_____

_____

TODAY IS _____ , 20 ____

I am grateful

_____

_____

I am grateful

_____

_____

I am grateful

_____

_____

I am grateful

_____

_____

⭐ TODAY IS _____ , 20 ___

No Writing today. DraW a picture of What you are grateful for.

☀ TODAY IS _____ , 20 ___

I am grateful

_____

_____

I am grateful

_____

_____

I am grateful

_____

_____

I am grateful

_____

_____

 TODAY IS _____ , 20 ____

I am grateful

_____

_____

I am grateful

_____

_____

I am grateful

_____

_____

I am grateful

_____

_____

TODAY IS _____ , 20 ___

No writing today. Draw a picture of what you are grateful for.

 TODAY IS _____ , 20 ____

I am grateful

_____

_____

I am grateful

_____

_____

I am grateful

_____

_____

I am grateful

_____

_____

TODAY IS _____ , 20 ____

I am grateful

_____

_____

I am grateful

_____

_____

I am grateful

_____

_____

I am grateful

_____

_____

 TODAY IS _____ , 20 _____

I am grateful

_____

_____

I am grateful

_____

_____

I am grateful

_____

_____

I am grateful

_____

_____

☀ TODAY IS   , 20

I am grateful

_____

_____

I am grateful

_____

_____

I am grateful

_____

_____

I am grateful

_____

_____

✿ TODAY IS _____ , 20 ___

No writing today. Draw a picture of what you are grateful for.

TODAY IS _____ , 20 ____

I am grateful

_____

_____

I am grateful

_____

_____

I am grateful

_____

_____

I am grateful

_____

_____

TODAY IS _____ , 20 ____

I am grateful

_____

_____

I am grateful

_____

_____

I am grateful

_____

_____

I am grateful

_____

_____

☆ TODAY IS _____ , 20 ____

No Writing today. Draw a picture of What you are grateful for.

☀ TODAY IS _____ , 20

I am grateful

_____

_____

I am grateful

_____

_____

I am grateful

_____

_____

I am grateful

_____

_____

☀ TODAY IS _____ , 20 ___

I am grateful
_____

_____

I am grateful
_____

_____

I am grateful
_____

_____

I am grateful
_____

_____

☼ TODAY IS _____ , 20 _____

No writing today. Draw a picture of what you are grateful for.

�❀ TODAY IS _____ , 20 ____

I am grateful

_____

_____

I am grateful

_____

_____

I am grateful

_____

_____

I am grateful

_____

_____

TODAY IS _____ , 20 ____

I am grateful

_____

_____

I am grateful

_____

_____

I am grateful

_____

_____

I am grateful

_____

_____

MY FIRST GRATITUDE JOURNAL

☆ TODAY IS _____ , 20 _____

No Writing today. Draw a picture of what you are grateful for.

☀ TODAY IS _____ , 20

I am grateful

_____

_____

I am grateful

_____

_____

I am grateful

_____

_____

I am grateful

_____

_____

I am grateful for YOU.

Vivian

OTHER BOOKS BY VIVIAN TENORIO:

Pink Slip to Product Launch in a Weak Economy

Pregnancy Journal: heartwarming memories

High School Journal: 4-year journal of my high school years

Wisdom Journal: wisdom worth passing on

Dating Journal: remember why you fell in love

2012 - 2016 Gratitude Journal: magical moments should be
remembered ever

2012 - 2016 Dream Journal: remember your dreams ever

My Law of Attraction Journal

EN ESPAÑOL

Diario de Embarazo: tiernos recuerdos

2012 – 2016 Diario de Gratitud: los momentos mágicos deben
ser recordados

2012 – 2016 Diario de Sueños: recuerde sus suenos para
siempre

40831004R00063

Made in the USA
Middletown, DE
24 February 2017